CALENDAR SKILLS

SUMMER CELEBRATIONS

by Marilynn G. Barr

Publisher: Roberta Suid

Production: Little Acorn & Associates, Inc.

SUMMER CELEBRATIONS
Entire contents copyright © 2004
by Monday Morning Books, Inc.

For a complete catalog, write to the address below:
Monday Morning Books, Inc.
PO Box 1134
Inverness, CA 94937

Call our toll-free number: 1-800-255-6049
E-mail us at: MMBooks@aol.com
Visit our Web site:
http://www.mondaymorningbooks.com

ISBN 1-57612-214-X

Printed in the United States of America
9 8 7 6 5 4 3 2 1

Contents

Introduction

Summer Celebrations features skills-practice activities and projects for 15 unique celebrations that occur during the months of June, July, and August. Five summer celebrations, per month, are listed at the top of each two-page programmable monthly calendar. Also featured is a game board with playing pieces. Celebrations include hands-on matching, sorting, or counting activities, booklets, and craft projects designed to encourage and reinforce individual creativity.

All activities and craft projects include a materials list, directions, and easy-to-cut out patterns. Prepare activities in advance for use in skills practice centers or reproduce and provide patterns and materials for take-home projects. Craft materials include items such as pom poms, glitter, ribbon, yarn, buttons, beans, beads, stickers, and drinking straws.

Children will practice matching, sorting, and counting skills as they fill ice cream soda glasses with matching ice cream scoops and make ice cream soda counting booklets during Ice Cream Soda Days. For a perfect ending to your Ice Cream Soda Days, provide children with ice cream soda glasses and scoops (pages 11-12), crayons, scissors, spaghetti noodles, beads, small pom poms, and plastic straws to assemble Ice Cream Soda Surprise displays. Post finished projects on a display board.

Calendars

Reproduce, color, cut out, and laminate a two-page calendar (pages 5-6, 25-26, 45-46). Use removable stickers or an erasable crayon or marker to program. Block two to three days or an entire week for each celebration on the calendar. Then program other activities and events such as birthdays, field trips, play dates, and scheduled visitors.

Game Boards and Game Pieces

Summer Celebrations features three game boards with matching game pieces. Games are designed to offer counting, matching, and sorting practice as well as the opportunity for children to develop their social and fair play skills. To play, players each choose a pawn. Each player, in turn, will roll a die, spin, or draw a card to determine how many spaces to move. Identify and explain consequence and bonus spaces to nonreaders and younger children.

Game Boards

Reproduce, color, cut out, and glue each game board half, matching the center seam, onto a sheet of oak tag or poster board. Then laminate.

Game Pieces

Die: Reproduce, color, and cut out the die pattern. Fold the pattern where indicated. Apply glue and secure each tab as you assemble the die.

Spinner: Reproduce, color, and cut out the spinner. Punch a hole in the center of the spinner, arrow, and where indicated on the game board and attach with a brass fastener.

Playing Cards: Reproduce, color, laminate, and cut cards apart.

Pawns: Reproduce, color, and cut out the pawn patterns. Fold each pattern where indicated and secure with glue, tape, or a staple.

JUNE IS FOR

DONUTS
ICE CREAM
FISHING
WATERMELONS
HOT AIR BALLOONS

SUNDAY	MONDAY	TUESDAY	WEDNESDAY	THURSDAY	FRIDAY	SATURDAY

Donut Concentration

Materials:

crayons or markers, scissors, glue, oak tag, envelope, plastic bag

Reproduce, color, cut out, and glue a donut box (page 8) onto a sheet of oak tag. Then laminate the donut box to use as a playing surface. Reproduce, color, laminate, and cut out donut cards (page 9). Glue an envelope to the back of the box for donut storage. Show how to shuffle and place all the donut cards, face down, on the donut box. Then have each player, in turn, turn over two cards to find a match. If there is a match, the player keeps the cards. If there is no match, the cards are turned back over, and the next player takes his or her turn. Play continues until all cards are matched.

Counting Donuts in a Box

Materials:

construction paper, crayons or markers, scissors, glue, stapler

Reproduce and cut out 55 donuts (page 9) for each child. Program, then reproduce ten donut boxes (page 8) with one numeral (1-10) written on each box for each child. After a discussion about number 1, provide each child with a donut box to color, cut out, and glue onto a sheet of construction paper. Then instruct children to count and glue the matching number of donuts onto their boxes. Repeat this for each remaining numeral. Provide an additional donut box (page 8) for each child to make a cover. Stack each child's set of boxes in sequence and staple to form a Counting Donuts in a Box booklet. Write each child's name on the front of his or her booklet.

Decorate-a-Donut

Materials:

crayons or markers, scissors, glue, construction paper, glitter, yarn scraps, beads, pom poms

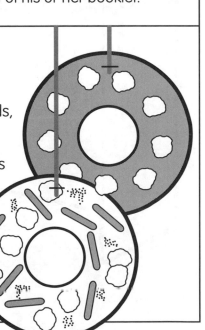

Prepare a work station with the materials listed above. Display decorated donuts as examples to get children started. Provide each child with a large colored construction paper donut (page 9) to cut out and decorate. Encourage children to be creative. Staple yarn to each finished donut to hang from door and window casings or from the ceiling. Write each child's name on the front of his or her donut.

Donut Days

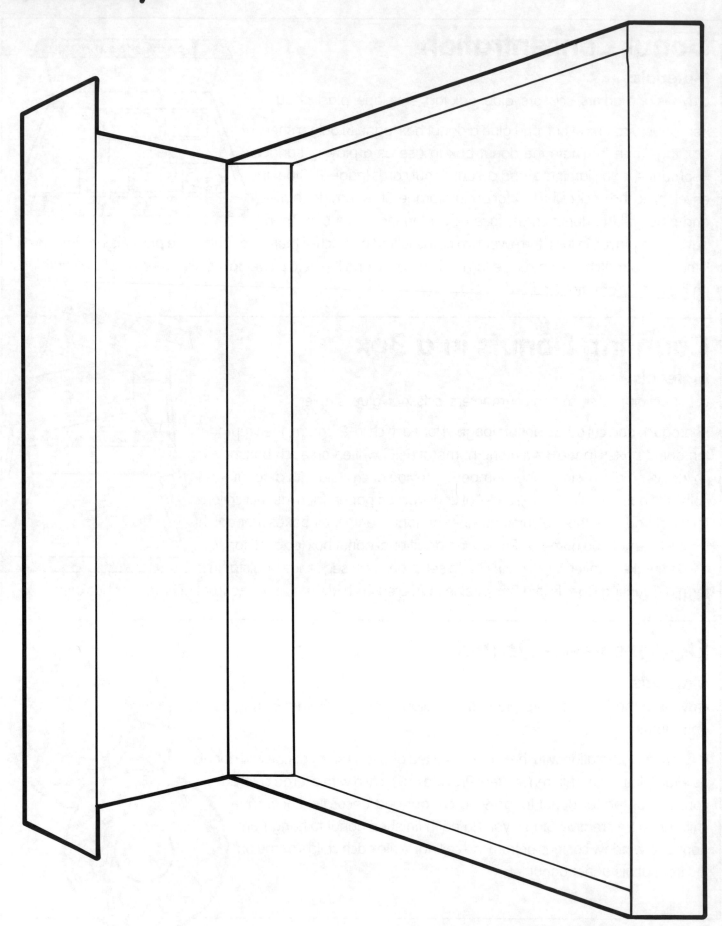

Donut Days

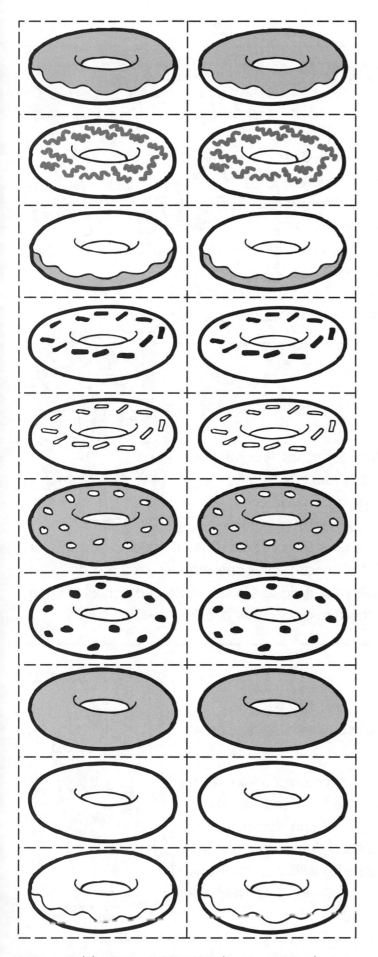

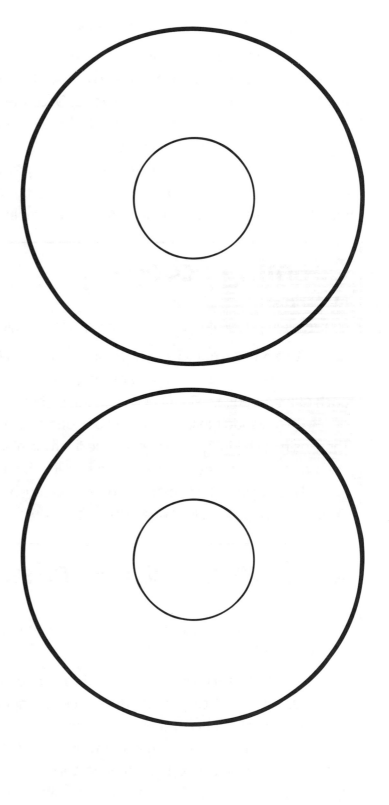

Ice Cream Soda Days

Ice Cream Soda Pattern Match

Materials:

crayons or markers, scissors, glue, folder, envelope

Reproduce, color, and cut out two ice cream sodas (page 11). Glue the sodas inside a folder (one on each side). Glue an envelope to the back of the folder for scoops storage. Decorate, then write Ice Cream Soda Pattern Match on the front of the folder. Reproduce, color, laminate, and cut out the patterned ice cream scoops (page 12) and place them inside the envelope on the back of the folder. To practice matching, children remove all scoops from the envelope, then fill the ice cream soda glasses with matching scoops. Program blank ice cream scoops (page 12) with numerals and number sets for a number skills practice activity.

Counting Scoops

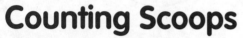

Materials:

construction paper, crayons or markers, scissors, glue, stapler

Reproduce and cut out 55 ice cream scoops (page 12) for each child. Program, then reproduce ten ice cream soda glasses (page 11) with one numeral (1-10) written on each glass for each child. After a discussion about number 1, provide each child with an ice cream soda glass to color, cut out, and glue onto a sheet of construction paper. Then instruct children to count and glue the matching number of scoops onto their glasses. Repeat this for each remaining numeral. Provide an additional sheet of construction paper and ice cream soda glass (page 11) for each child to make a cover. Stack each child's set of glasses in sequence and staple to form a Counting Scoops booklet. Write each child's name on the front of his or her booklet.

Ice Cream Soda Surprise

Materials:

crayons or markers, scissors, glue, construction paper, spaghetti noodles, beads, pom poms, plastic drinking straws

Provide each child with an ice cream soda and colored construction paper ice cream scoops (pages 11-12), crayons, scissors, broken spaghetti noodles, beads, small pom poms, and plastic drinking straws. Have children color, cut out, and glue their sodas onto sheets of construction paper. Then have them cut out and glue ice cream scoops onto their sodas. Encourage children to decorate their sodas with "marshmallow" pom poms or "spaghetti" sprinkles. Cut plastic drinking straws for children to glue onto their sodas. Post finished projects on a display board.

Ice Cream Soda Days

Ice Cream Soda Days

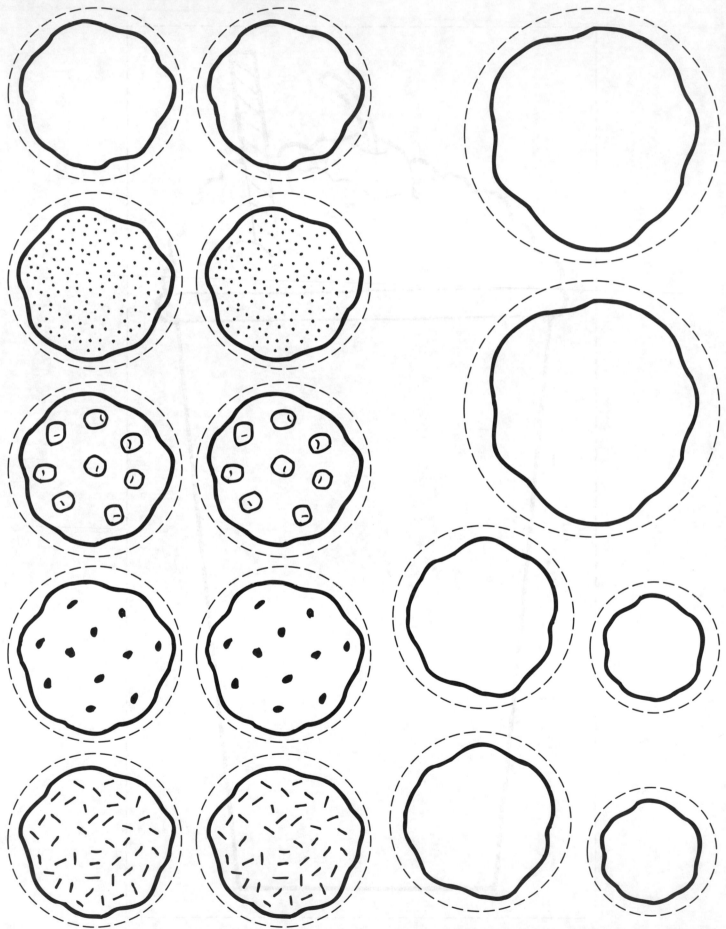

Matching Fish

Materials:

oak tag, crayons or markers, scissors, glue, envelope

Reproduce, color, cut out, and glue six fish bowls (page 14) onto separate sheets of oak tag. Write one color word (red, blue, yellow, green, purple, orange) on each bowl, then laminate to use as a playing surface. Reproduce, color, laminate, and cut apart fish cards (page 14) in matching colors. Glue an envelope to the back of one bowl for fish card storage. To practice matching colors, children remove all cards from the envelope to sort and place fish on matching color word fish bowls.

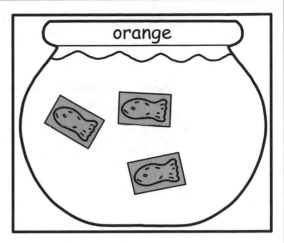

Counting Scales on a Fish

Materials:

construction paper, crayons or markers, scissors, glue, stapler

Reproduce and cut out 55 scale cards (page 15) for each child. Program ten construction paper fish (page 15) with one numeral (1-10) written on each fish tail for each child. Glue each fish onto a separate sheet of construction paper. After a

discussion about number 1, instruct children to count and glue a matching number of scales onto the fish. Repeat this for each remaining numeral. Provide an additional construction paper fish for each child to make a cover. Stack each child's set of fish sheets in sequence and staple to form a Counting Scales on a Fish booklet. Write each child's name on the front of his or her booklet.

Goldfish Bowls

Materials:

construction paper, crayons or markers, scissors, oak tag, glue, sand, glitter

Prepare a work station with the materials listed above. Provide each child with a construction paper fish bowl (page 14) to color, decorate, cut out, and glue onto a sheet of oak tag. Reproduce fish (page 14) for children to color, cut out, and glue to their bowls. Help each child write his or her name at the top of the bowl. Display finished work on a board entitled Our Goldfish Bowls.

Fishing Days

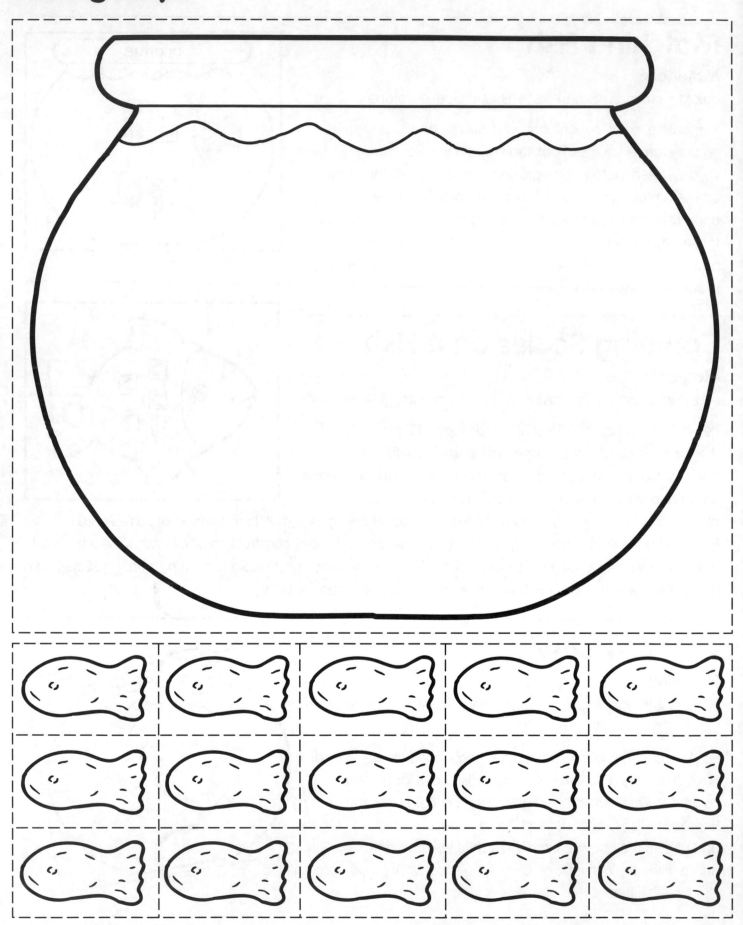

Watermelon Days

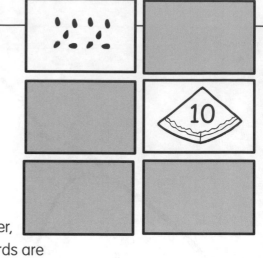

Matching Slices and Seeds

Materials:

construction paper, crayons or markers, scissors, plastic bag

Reproduce, color, laminate, and cut apart watermelon slice and seed set cards (page 17). Show how to shuffle and place all the cards, face down, on a flat surface. Then have each player, in turn, turn over two cards to find a match. If there is a match, the player keeps the cards. If there is no match, the cards are turned back over, and the next player takes his or her turn. Play continues until all cards are matched. Store cards in a resealable plastic bag when not in use. Reproduce a set of cards for each child for a take-home matching activity.

Drawing Watermelon Seeds

Materials:

construction paper, crayons or markers, scissors, glue, stapler

Reproduce, then program ten sheets of construction paper with watermelons (page 18) and a numeral sentence (1-10) as shown for each child. After a discussion about number 1, instruct children to draw the matching number of seeds on the watermelon. Repeat this for each remaining numeral. Provide an additional sheet of construction paper and watermelon (page 18) for each child to make a cover. Stack each child's set of watermelon pages in sequence and staple to form a Drawing Watermelon Seeds booklet. Write each child's name on the front of his or her booklet.

There are 10 seeds in the watermelon.

Paper Plate Watermelon Puzzle

Materials:

paper plate, construction paper, scissors, glue, crayons or markers, resealable plastic bags

Prepare a work station with the materials listed above. Have children color a paper plate to resemble a sliced watermelon. Then help each child cut his or her watermelon into four slices. Children practice matching the watermelon slices. Provide each child with a resealable plastic bag to store their watermelon slices.

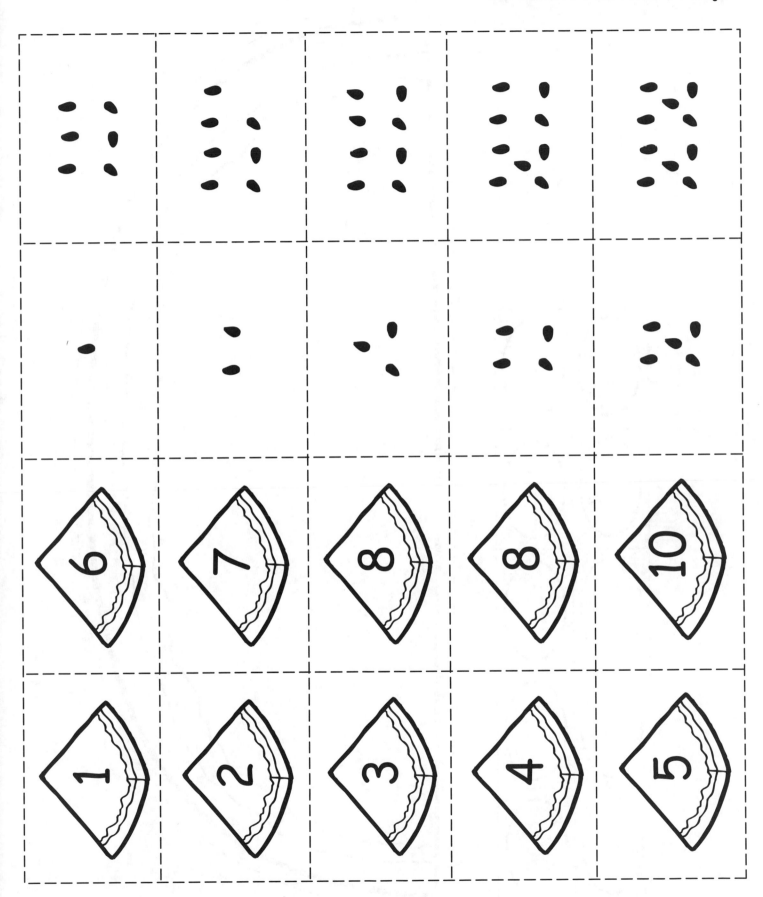

Watermelon Days

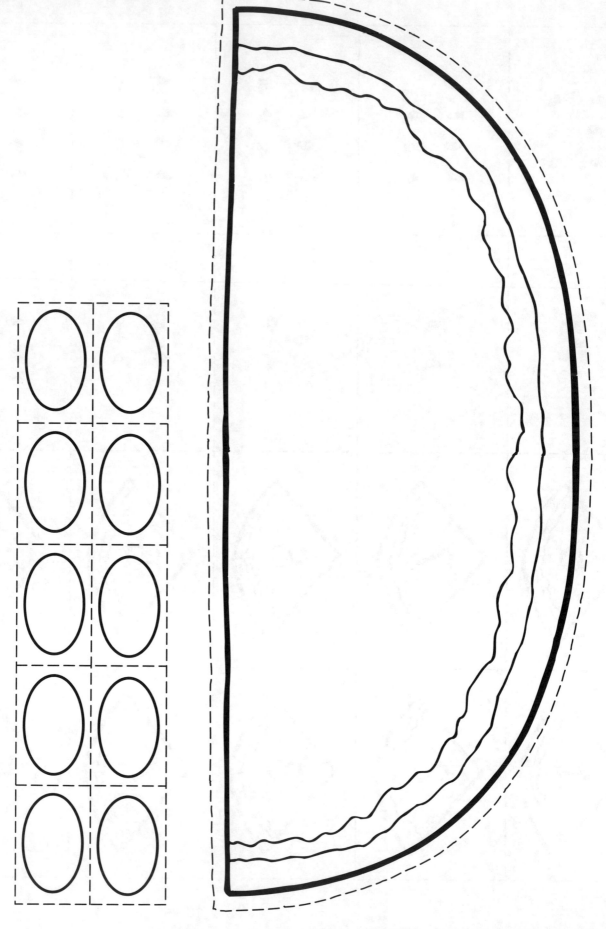

Matching Hot Air Balloons

Materials:

oak tag, crayons or markers, scissors, envelope

Reproduce, color, cut apart, and laminate two sets of large construction paper hot air balloon cards (page 20). Decorate an envelope for children to use as a playing surface and to store cards. Write Matching Hot Air Balloons on the front of the envelope. To practice matching patterns, children remove all cards from the envelope to sort and place matching sets on the envelope playing surface.

Hot Air Balloons in the Sky

Materials:

construction paper, crayons or markers, scissors, glue, stapler

There are 2 hot air balloons in the sky.

Reproduce and cut out 55 small balloon cards (page 20) for each child. Reproduce, then program ten sheets of construction paper with clouds and a numeral sentence (1-10) as shown for each child. After a discussion about number 1, instruct children to count and glue a matching number of hot air balloons in the sky. Repeat this for each remaining numeral. Provide an additional sheet of construction paper for each child to decorate a cover. Stack each child's cover and set of balloon pages in sequence and staple to form a Hot Air Balloons in the Sky booklet. Write each child's name on the front of his or her booklet.

My Hot Air Balloon Adventure

Materials:

construction paper, crayons or markers, scissors, glue, glitter, buttons, pom poms, cotton balls, star stickers, yarn

Prepare a work station with the supplies listed above. Provide each child with a set of hot air balloon patterns (page 21) to color and cut out. Have children decorate their hot air balloons. Help each cut and staple two lengths of yarn to attach the balloon to the basket. Have each child glue his or her cat or dog onto the basket. Invite children, in turn, to share a story about his or her hot air balloon adventure.

Hot Air Balloon Days

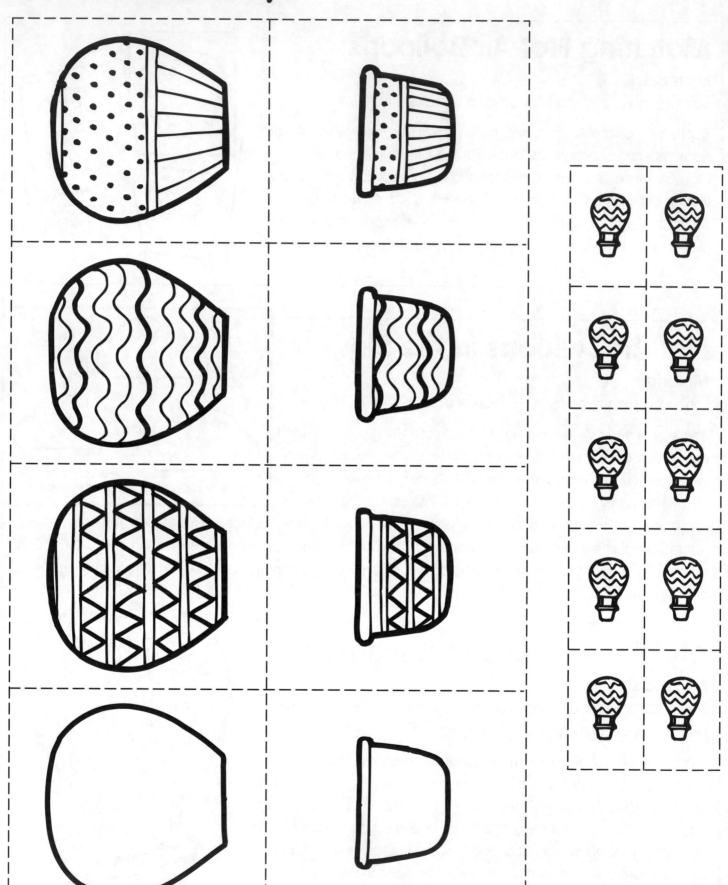

MATCH-A-SHAPE
BALLOONS

June Game Pieces

Reproduce, color, cut out, and glue each game board half (pages 22-23), matching the center seam, onto a sheet of oak tag or poster board, then laminate. Reproduce, color, and cut out shapes. To play, children take turns sorting and placing each shape on a matching hot air balloon.

JULY IS FOR
ICE CREAM
KOALAS
PICNICS
TURTLE RACES
BLUEBERRIES

SUNDAY	MONDAY	TUESDAY	WEDNESDAY	THURSDAY	FRIDAY	SATURDAY

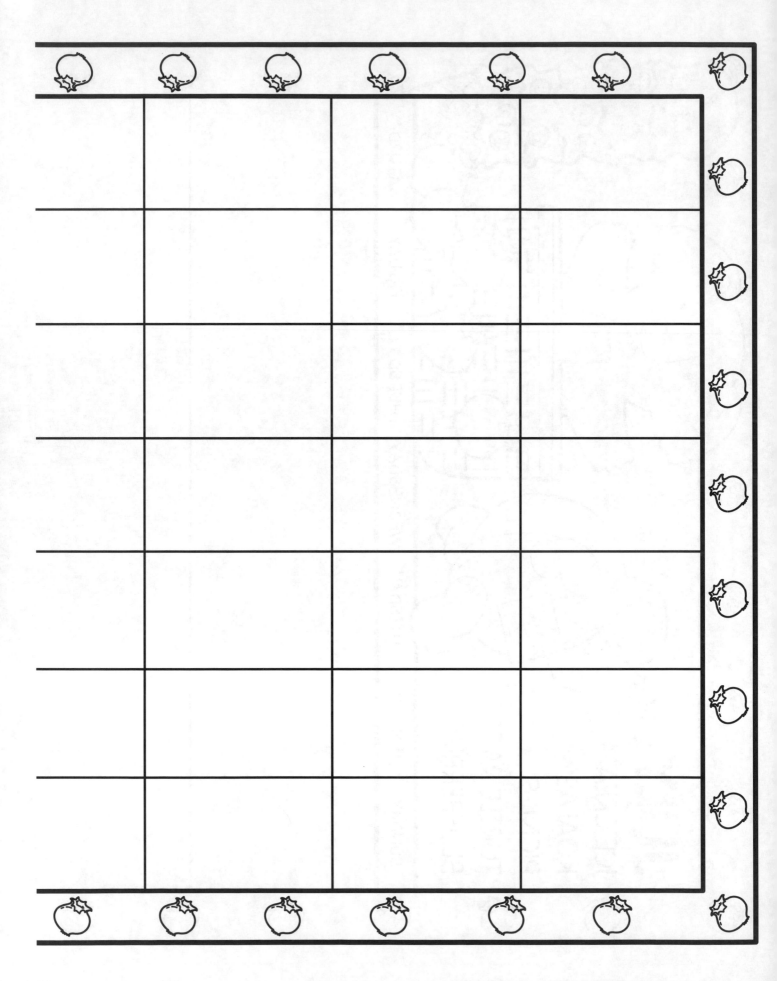

Matching Ice Cream Cones

Materials:

oak tag, crayons or markers, scissors, envelope

Reproduce and cut apart six large single scoop construction paper cones and six ice cream scoops (page 29). Program cones with color words (red, blue, yellow, green, orange, purple) and color scoops with matching colored crayons. Then laminate and cut apart. Decorate an envelope for children to use as a playing surface and to store cones and scoops. Write Matching Ice Cream Cones on the front of the envelope. To practice matching colors to color words, children remove all scoops and cones from the envelope to sort and place matching sets on the envelope playing surface.

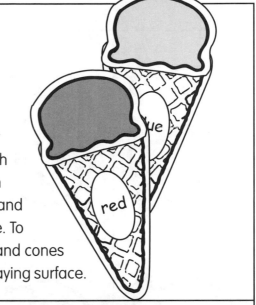

Ice Cream Concentration

Materials:

construction paper, crayons or markers, scissors, plastic bag

Reproduce, color, laminate, and cut apart construction paper ice cream cards (page 28). Show how to shuffle and place all the cards, face down, on a flat surface. Then have each player, in turn, turn over two cards to find a match. If there is a match, the player keeps the cards. If there is no match, the cards are turned back over, and the next player takes his or her turn. Play continues until all cards are matched. Store cards in a resealable plastic bag when not in use. Reproduce a set of cards for each child for a take-home matching activity.

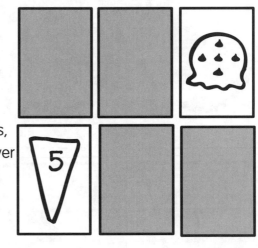

Ice Cream Creations

Materials:

oak tag, construction paper, crayons or markers, scissors, glue, pom poms, glitter, beans, beads, yarn scraps

Prepare a work station with a variety of craft materials for children to make Ice Cream Creations. Provide each child with a cone (page 29) of his or her choice and scoops (page 29) to color and cut out. Encourage children to be creative as they build their ice cream creations. Glue finished ice cream cones onto oak tag. Help each child write his or her name on the cones. Mount finished work on a bulletin board entitled Our Ice Cream Creations.

Ice Cream Days

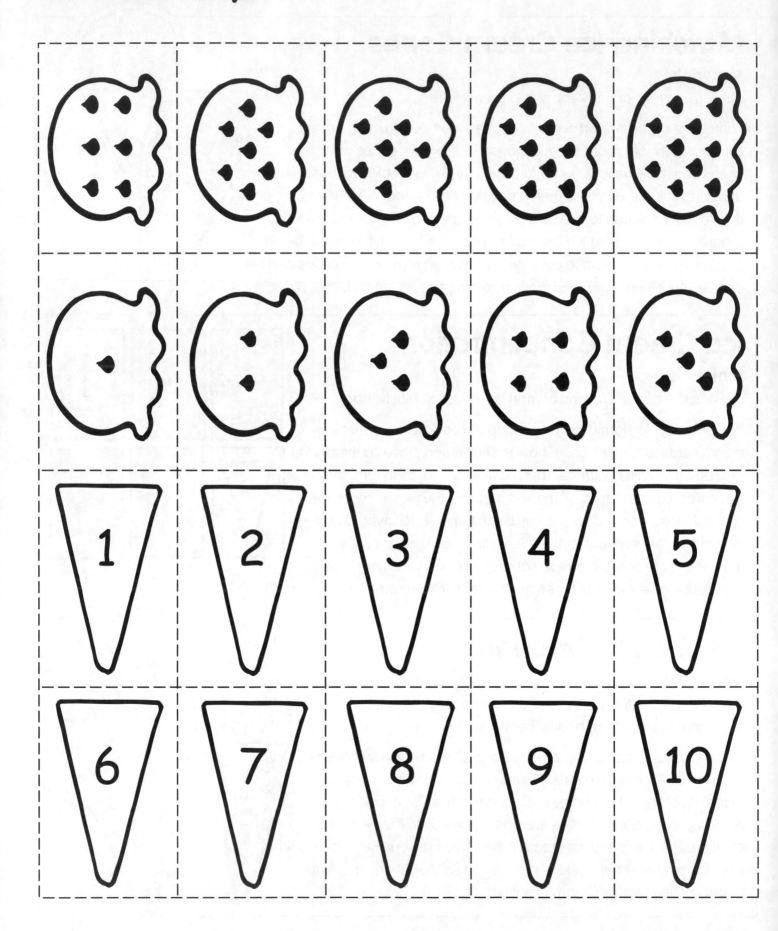

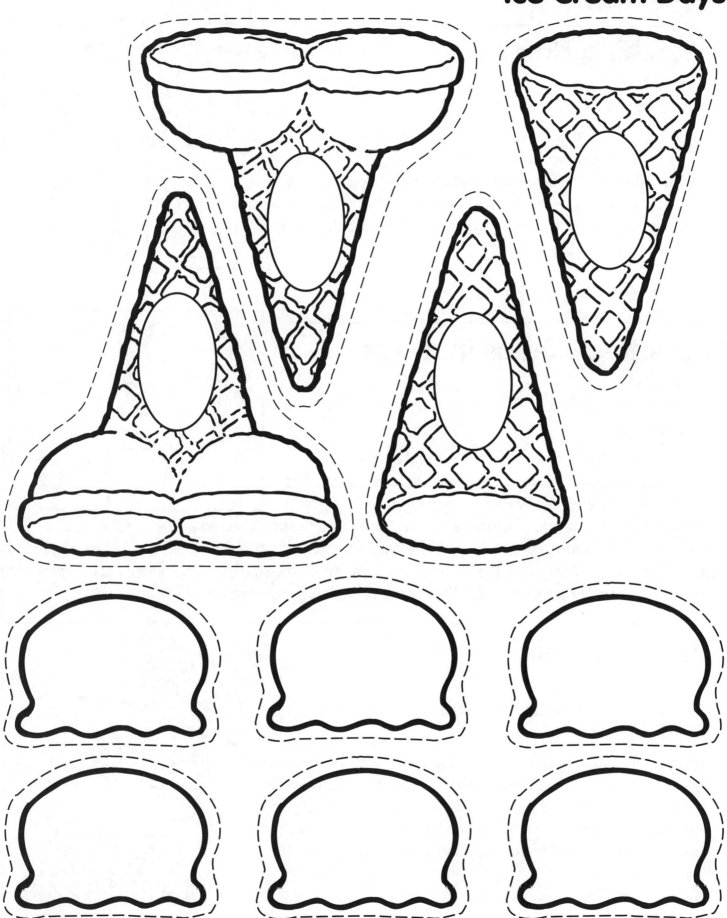

Koala Days

Matching Koalas

Materials:

oak tag, crayons or markers, scissors, envelope

Reproduce, color, cut apart, and laminate large construction koalas (page 31). Decorate an envelope for children to use as a playing surface and to store cards. Write Matching Koalas on the front of the envelope. To practice matching directional koalas, children remove all cards from the envelope to sort and place matching sets on the envelope playing surface.

Counting Koalas in a Tree

I see one koala in the tree.

Materials:

oak tag, construction paper, crayons or markers, scissors, glue, envelope

Provide each child with a sheet of oak tag and an envelope for storage. Have children decorate their envelopes with crayons or markers. Help each child write Counting Koalas In a Tree on the front of his or her envelope. Reproduce ten small koalas (page 31) for children to color and cut apart. Pretend you are koala watching in Australia. Invite each child, in turn, to ask "How many koalas do you see?" Give a number from 1-10. Then have children count and place the matching number of koalas on each of their trees. Check each child's tree before you sight any more koalas.

Dress a Koala

Materials:

wallpaper or gift wrap scraps, felt, colored construction paper, scissors, oak tag, envelopes

Provide each child with an oak tag koala (page 32). Have children color and cut out their koalas. Reproduce koala clothes (page 32) templates for children to use to cut out matching shirts and pants from wallpaper, gift wrap, felt, and construction paper for their koalas. Provide an envelope for each child to decorate and store his or her koala and clothing patterns.

Koala Days

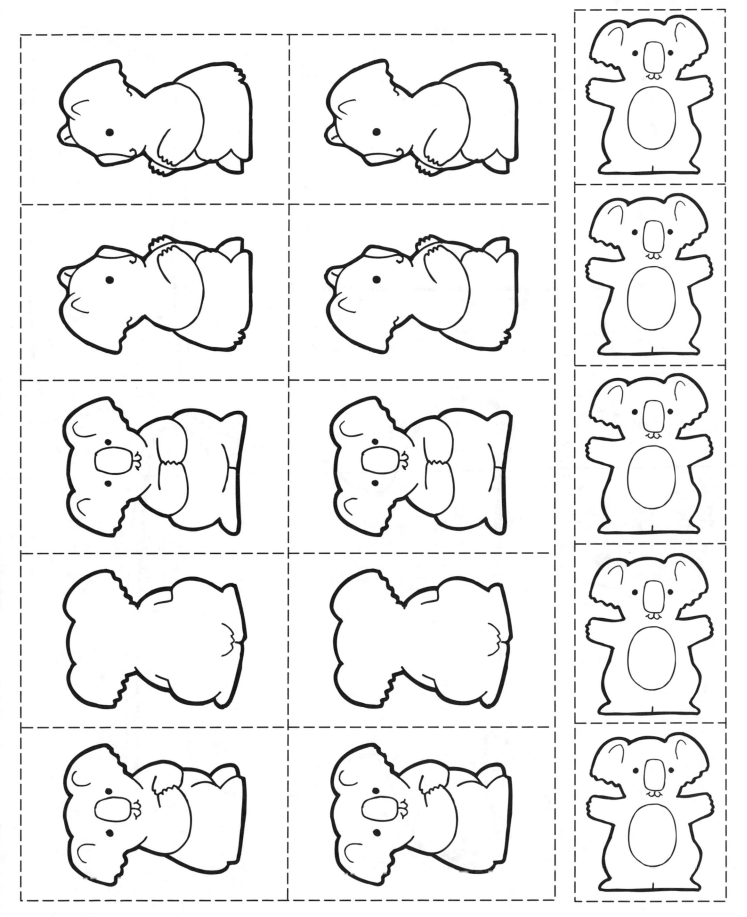

Koala Days

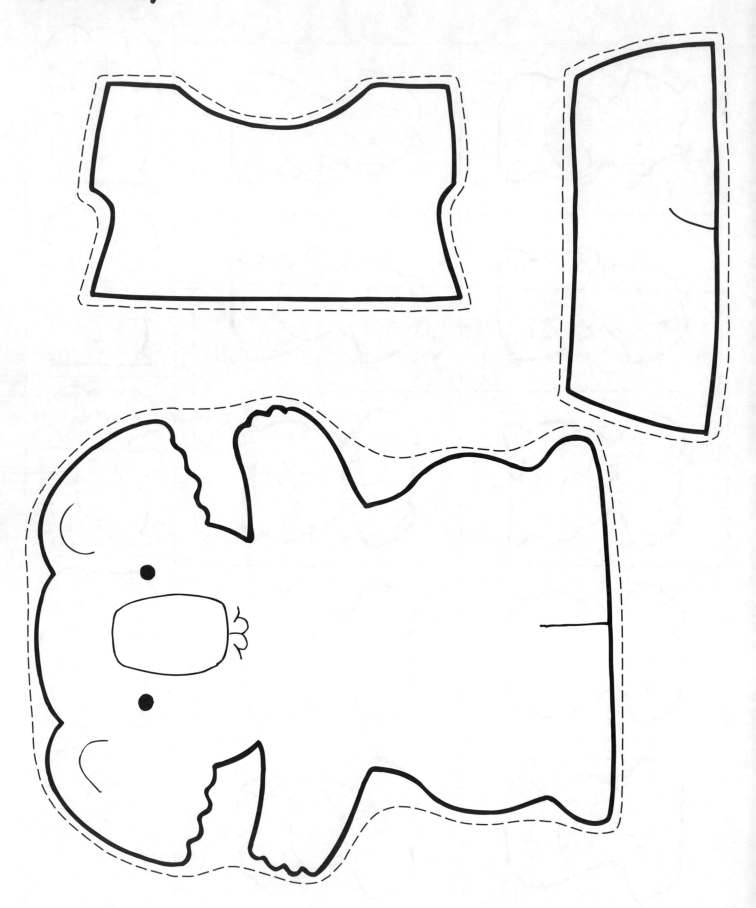

Summer Celebrations • ©2004 Monday Morning Books, Inc.

Picnic Food Match

Materials:

oak tag, crayons or markers, scissors, envelope

Reproduce, color, cut apart, and laminate two sets of construction paper picnic food cards (page 35). Decorate an envelope for children to use as a playing surface and to store cards. Write Picnic Food Match on the front of the envelope. To practice matching, children remove all cards from the envelope to sort and place matching sets on the envelope playing surface. Children can also use the cards to play a game of Picnic Food Concentration.

Counting Sandwiches

Materials:

construction paper, crayons or markers, scissors, plastic bag

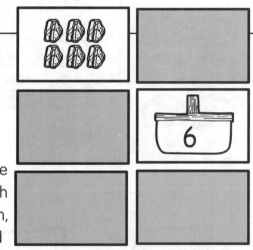

Reproduce, color, laminate, and cut apart construction paper sandwich set and picnic basket cards (page 34). Show how to shuffle and place all the cards, face down, on a flat surface. Then have each player, in turn, turn over two cards to find a match. If there is a match, the player keeps the cards. If there is no match, the cards are turned back over, and the next player takes his or her turn. Play continues until all cards are matched. Store cards in a resealable plastic bag when not in use. Reproduce a set of cards for each child for a take-home matching activity.

Packing For a Picnic

Materials:

construction paper, crayons or markers, scissors, glue

Reproduce picnic food patterns (page 35) for children to color and cut apart. Provide each child with an enlarged, picnic basket (page 35) to color and cut out. Have children glue food patterns onto their baskets. Mount finished picnic baskets on separate sheets of colored construction paper for display. Help each child write his or her name on his or her basket.

Picnic Days

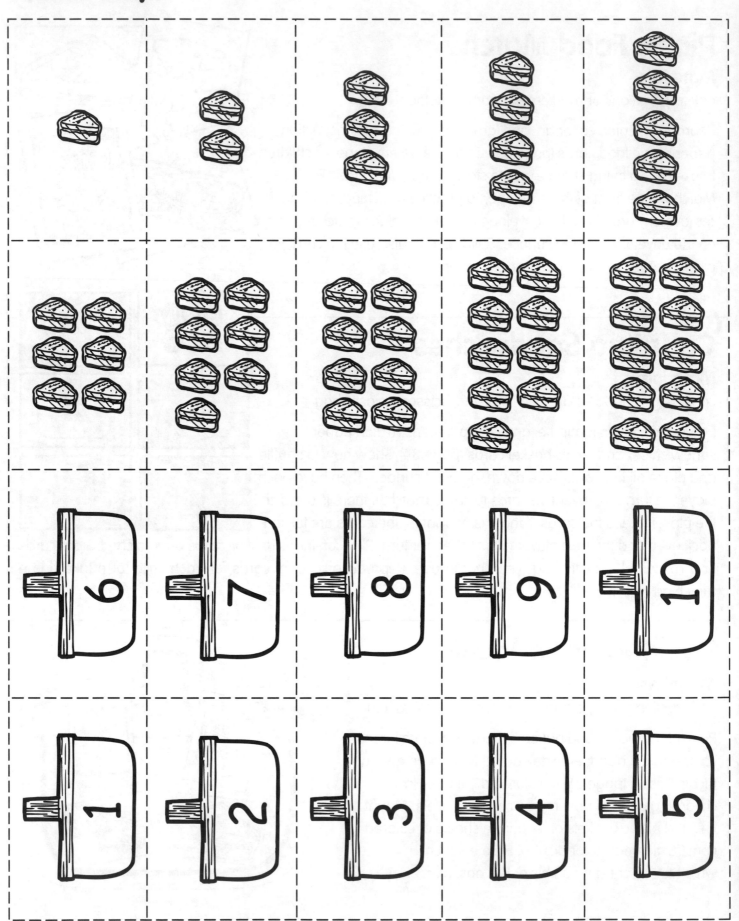

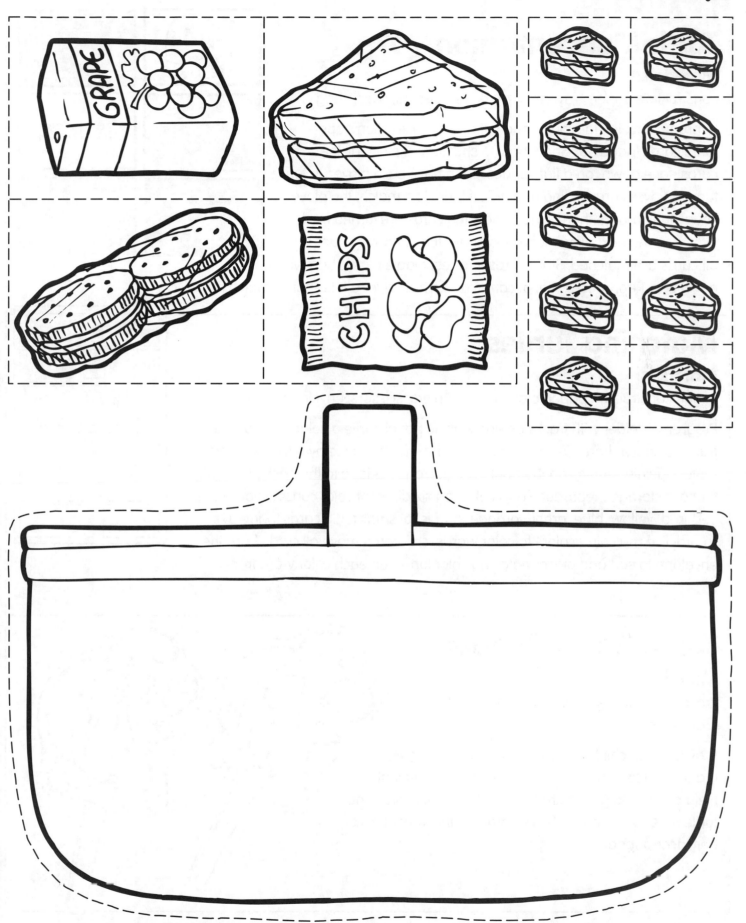

Turtle Race Days

Turtle Concentration

Materials:

construction paper, crayons or markers, scissors, plastic bag

Reproduce, color, laminate, and cut apart construction paper turtle cards (page 38). Show how to shuffle and place all the cards, face down, on a flat surface. Then have each player, in turn, turn over two cards to find a match. If there is a match, the player keeps the cards. If there is no match, the cards are turned back over, and the next player takes his or her turn. Play continues until all cards are matched. Store cards in a resealable plastic bag when not in use. Reproduce a set of cards for each child for a take-home matching activity.

Matching Turtles

Materials:

folder, construction paper, crayons or markers, scissors, envelope

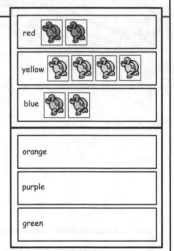

Program a folder with tracks on each inside panel. Write a color word on each track as shown here. Decorate the front of the folder with crayons or markers. Write Matching Turtles on the front and glue an envelope to the back of the folder for card storage. Reproduce and cut apart six different color construction paper sets (red, yellow, blue, green, orange, purple) of small turtle cards (page 37). To practice matching colors to color words, children remove all cards from the envelope to sort and place matching color turtles on each color word track.

Turtle Racer Puppet

Materials:

crayons or markers, scissors, oak tag, glue, craft sticks

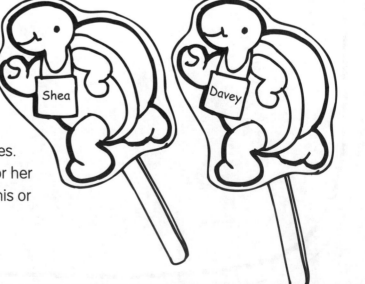

Provide each child with an oak tag turtle racer (page 37). Have children color and cut out their turtles. Help each child glue a craft stick to the back of his or her turtle racer. Write each child's name on the front of his or her racer puppet.

Turtle Race Days

Turtle Race Days

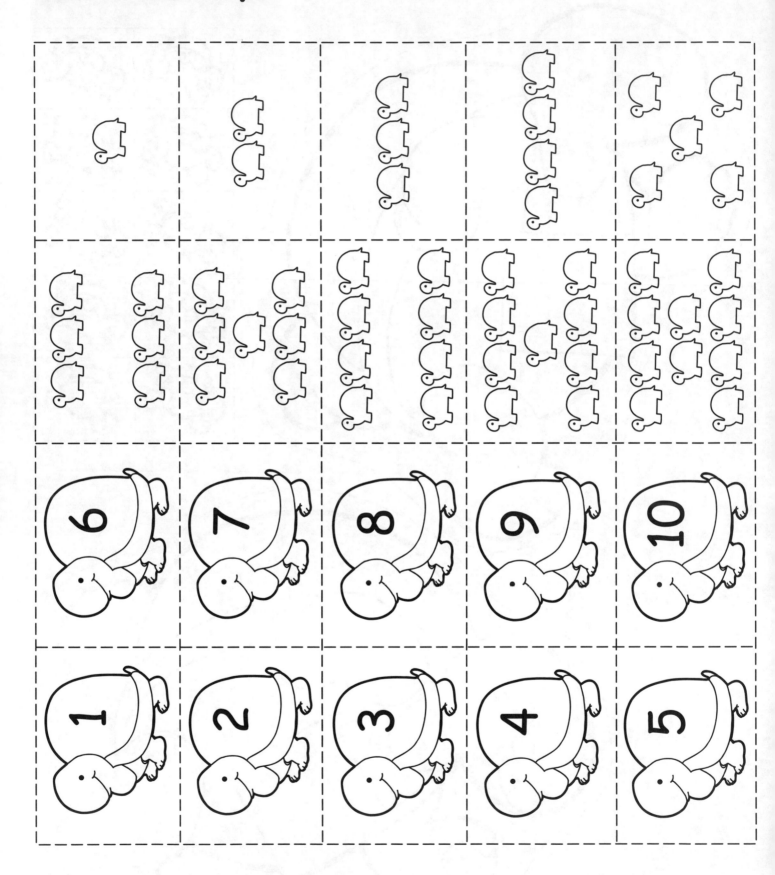

Blueberry Concentration

Materials:

construction paper, crayons or markers, scissors, plastic bag

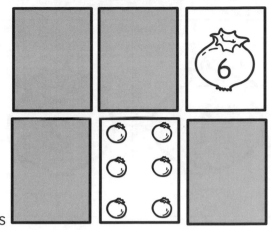

Reproduce, color, laminate, and cut apart construction paper blueberry cards (page 40). Show how to shuffle and place all the cards, face down, on a flat surface. Then have each player, in turn, turn over two cards to find a match. If there is a match, the player keeps the cards. If there is no match, the cards are turned back over, and the next player takes his or her turn. Play continues until all cards are matched. Store cards in a resealable plastic bag when not in use. Reproduce a set of cards for each child for a take-home matching and counting activity.

Counting Blueberries in a Pie

Materials:

construction paper, crayons or markers, scissors, glue, stapler

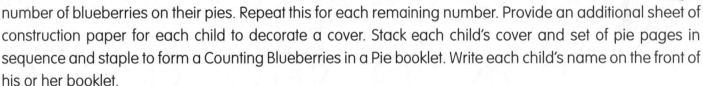

Reproduce and cut out 55 blueberry cards (page 41) for each child. Reproduce, then program ten construction paper pies (page 41) with a number word (one to ten) for each child. After a discussion about number 1, instruct children to count and glue the matching number of blueberries on their pies. Repeat this for each remaining number. Provide an additional sheet of construction paper for each child to decorate a cover. Stack each child's cover and set of pie pages in sequence and staple to form a Counting Blueberries in a Pie booklet. Write each child's name on the front of his or her booklet.

Blueberry Pom Pom Pies

Materials:

oak tag, crayons or markers, scissors, dark blue pom poms, glue

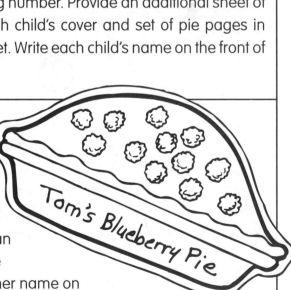

Prepare a work station with the materials listed above for children to use to make Blueberry Pom Pom Pies. Provide each child with an oak tag pie (page 41) to color and cut out. Then have children glue dark blue pom poms onto their pies. Help each child write his or her name on the pie dish. Mount finished pies on colored construction paper for display on a bulletin board entitled Blueberry Pom Pom Pies. Serve blueberries or blueberry pie as a snack.

Blueberry Days

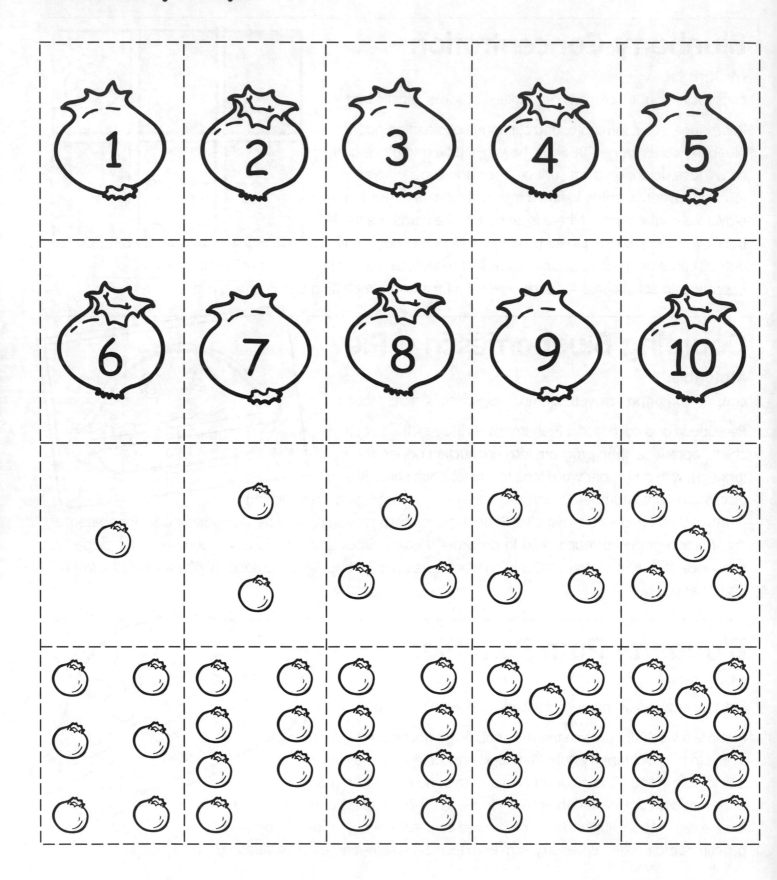

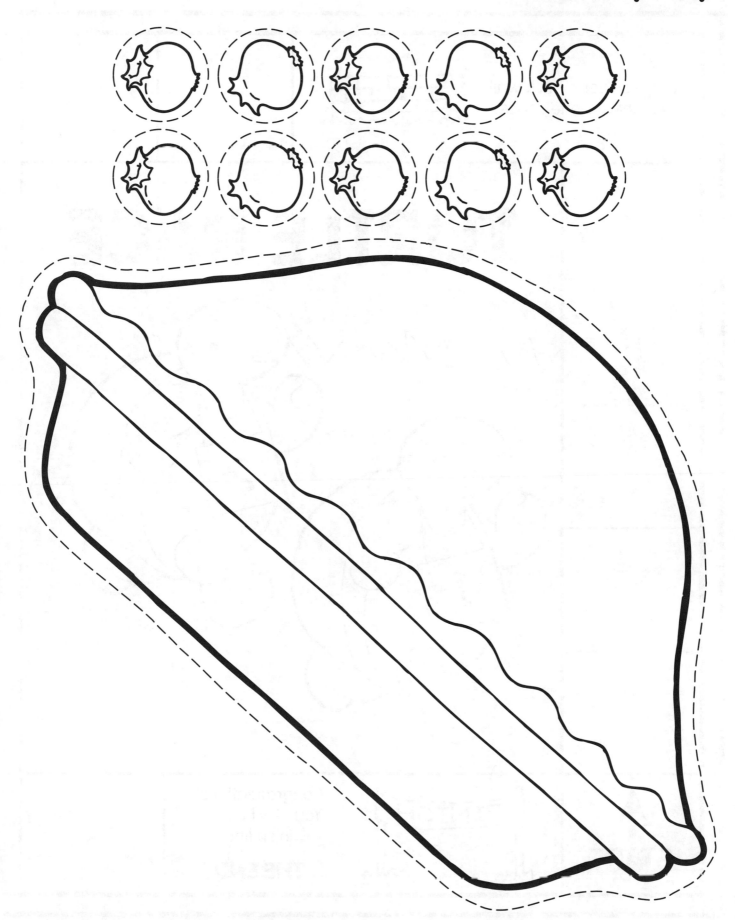

Jumped over a brick wall.
Go forward one space.

TURTLE RACE

↑
START

FINISH

Congratulations!
You reached the
finish line.

THE END

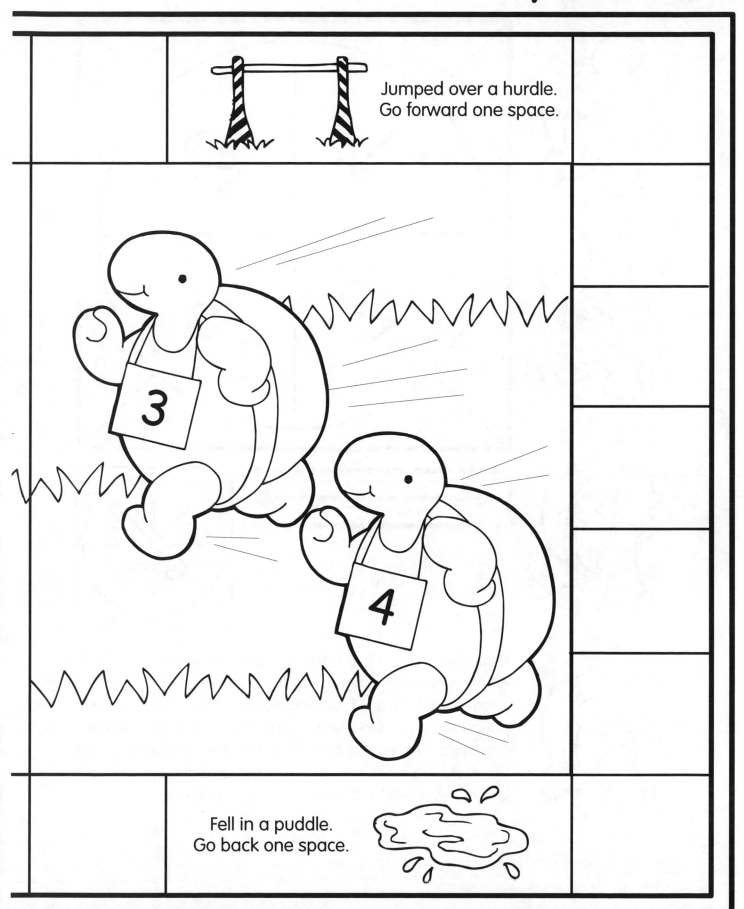

Jumped over a hurdle.
Go forward one space.

Fell in a puddle.
Go back one space.

July Game Pieces

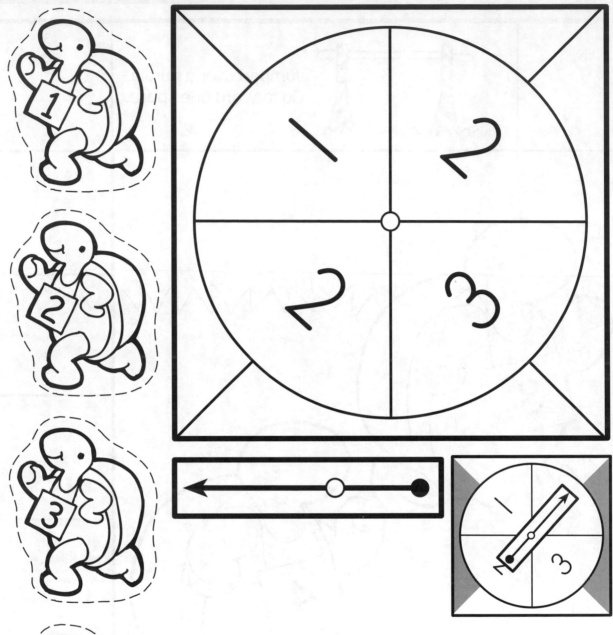

Reproduce, color, cut out, and glue each game board half (pages 42-43), matching the center seam, onto a sheet of oak tag or poster board, then laminate. Reproduce, color, and cut out turtle racer pawns and assemble spinner as shown. To play, each player, in turn, spins the arrow on the spinner, then moves his or her pawn the matching number of spaces shown on the spinner. Play continues until each player reaches the Finish line.

AUGUST IS FOR

PEACHES
CLOWNS
BANANAS
POPSICLES
HORSESHOES

SUNDAY	MONDAY	TUESDAY	WEDNESDAY	THURSDAY	FRIDAY	SATURDAY

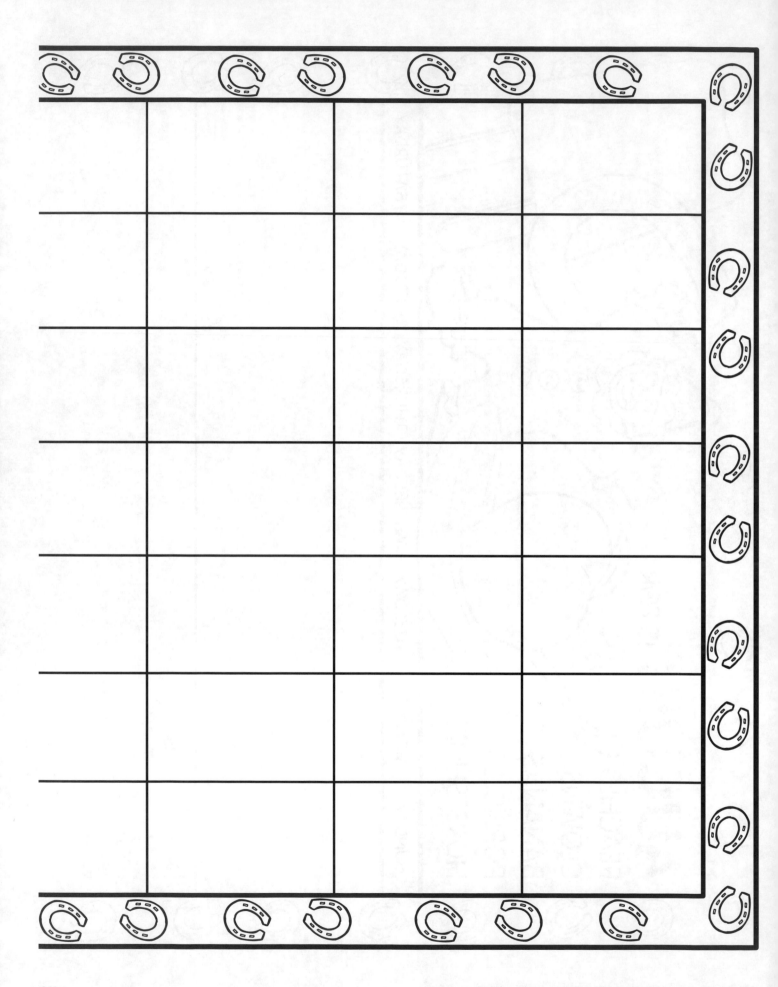

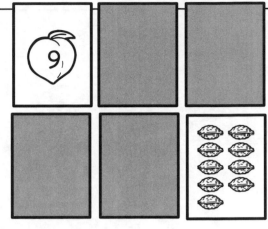

Peach Concentration

Materials:

construction paper, crayons or markers, scissors, plastic bag

Reproduce, color, laminate, and cut apart construction paper peach and pit cards (page 48). Show how to shuffle and place all the cards, face down, on a flat surface. Then have each player, in turn, turn over two cards to find a match. If there is a match, the player keeps the cards. If there is no match, the cards are turned back over, and the next player takes his or her turn. Play continues until all cards are matched. Store cards in a resealable plastic bag when not in use. Reproduce a set of cards for each child for a take-home matching activity.

Counting Pits on a Peach

Materials:

construction paper, crayons or markers, scissors, glue, stapler

Reproduce and cut out 55 peach pit cards (page 49) for each child. Program ten large construction paper peaches (page 49) with one numeral (1-10) written at the bottom of each peach for each child. After a discussion about number 1, instruct children to count and glue the matching number of pits on the peach. Repeat this for each remaining numeral. Provide an additional construction paper peach for each child to make a cover. Stack each child's set of peaches in sequence and staple to form a Counting Pits on a Peach booklet. Write each child's name on the front of his or her booklet.

Peach Mobile

Materials:

crayons or markers, scissors, glue, construction paper, stapler, yarn

Provide each child with a set of graduated-size, construction paper peaches (page 49) to color, cut out, and assemble. Staple each peach to a length of yarn as shown here. Hang finished peach mobiles from door and window casings or from the ceiling of an imaginary peach orchard. Write each child's name on the back of his or her mobile.

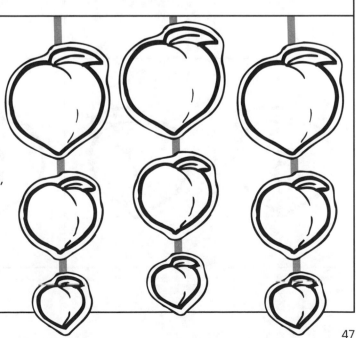

Peach Days

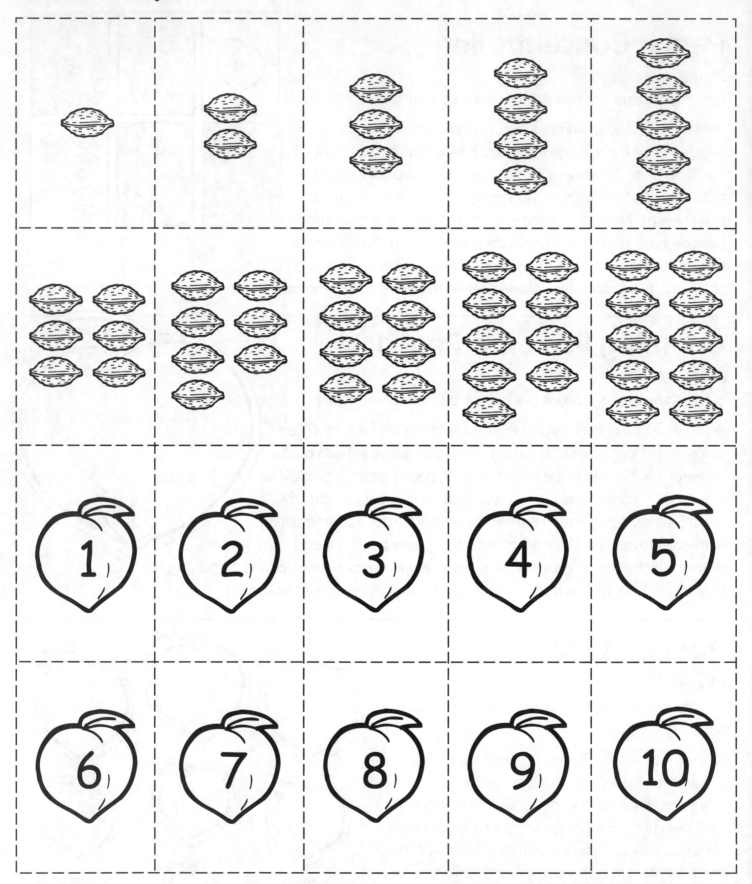

Peach Days

Clown Days

Matching Clowns

Materials:

folder, construction paper, scissors, glue, envelope

Reproduce, laminate, and cut apart two sets of oak tag clown cards (page 51). Glue one set to the inside of a folder. Decorate, then write Matching Clowns on the front of the folder. Glue an envelope to the back of the folder for clown card storage. To practice matching clowns, children remove all clown cards from the envelope to sort and place matching clown cards on the folder.

Counting Buttons on a Clown

Materials:

construction paper, crayons or markers, scissors, glue, stapler

Reproduce and cut out 55 button cards (page 51 for each child. Program ten construction paper clowns (page 52) with one numeral (1-10) written on each clown's hat for each child. After a discussion about number 1, instruct children to count and glue a matching number of buttons onto the clown. Repeat this for each remaining numeral. Provide an additional construction paper clown for each child to make a cover. Stack each child's set of clowns in sequence and staple to form a Counting Buttons on a Clown booklet. Write each child's name on the front of his or her booklet.

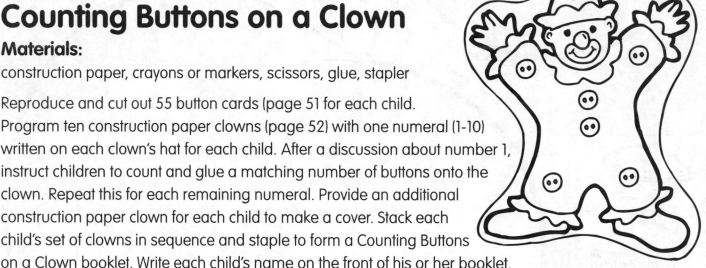

Clown Puppet

Materials:

crayons or markers, scissors, oak tag, glue, glitter, buttons, ribbons, yarn, craft sticks

Provide each child with an oak tag clown (page 52). Have children color, cut out, and decorate their clowns with a variety of craft materials. Help each child glue a craft stick to the back of his or her clown. Write each child's name on the front of his or her clown puppet.

Clown Days

Clown Days

Bananas and Bowls Concentration

Materials:

construction paper, crayons or markers, scissors, plastic bag

Reproduce, color, laminate, and cut apart a set of construction paper banana slice and bowl cards (page 55). Show how to shuffle and place all the cards, face down, on a flat surface. Then have each player, in turn, turn over two cards to find a match. If there is a match, the player keeps the cards. If there is no match, the cards are turned back over, and the next player takes his or her turn. Play continues until all cards are matched. Store cards in a resealable plastic bag when not in use. Reproduce a set of cards for each child for a take-home matching activity.

Counting Bananas in a Bowl

Materials:

construction paper, crayons or markers, scissors, glue, stapler

Reproduce and cut out 55 banana slice cards (page 54) for each child. Program ten construction paper bowls (page 54) with one number word (one to ten) written at the top of each bowl for each child. After a discussion about number 1, instruct children to count and glue the matching number of banana slice cards onto the bowl. Repeat this for each remaining numeral. Provide an additional construction paper bowl for each child to make a cover. Stack each child's set of bowls in sequence and staple to form a Counting Bananas in a Bowl booklet. Write each child's name on the front of his or her booklet.

Bunch of Bananas

Materials:

crayons or markers, scissors, oak tag, glue, brass fastener

Provide each child with ten oak tag banana patterns (page 54) programmed with number words and numerals as shown here. Have children color and cut out their bananas. Help each child punch a hole at the stem of each banana. To form a Bunch of Bananas number word and numeral booklet, thread a brass fastener through the hole in each banana.

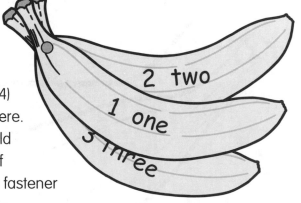

Banana Days

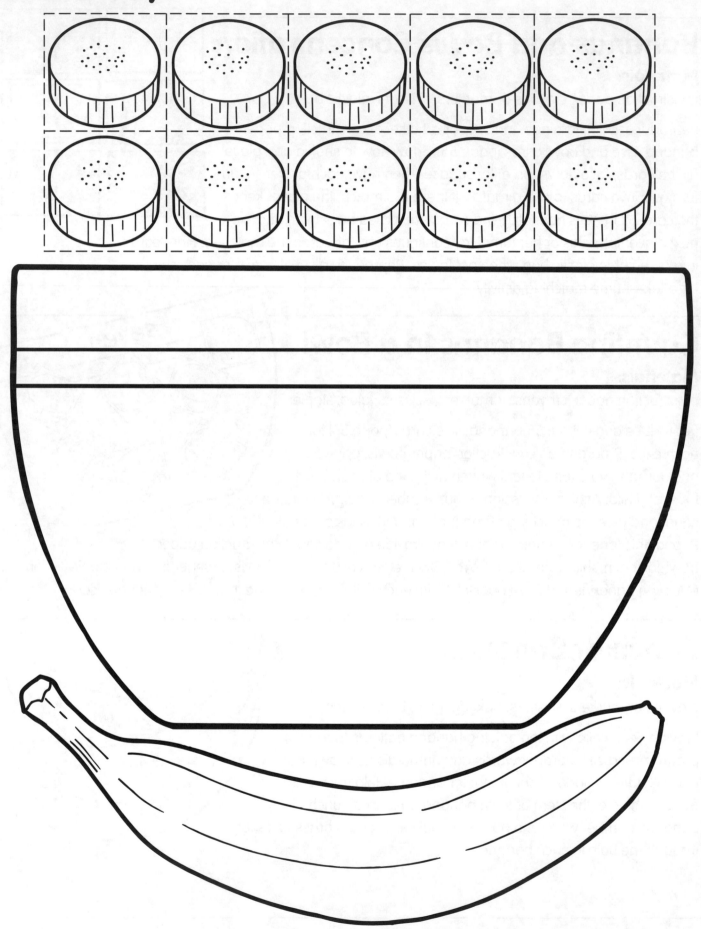

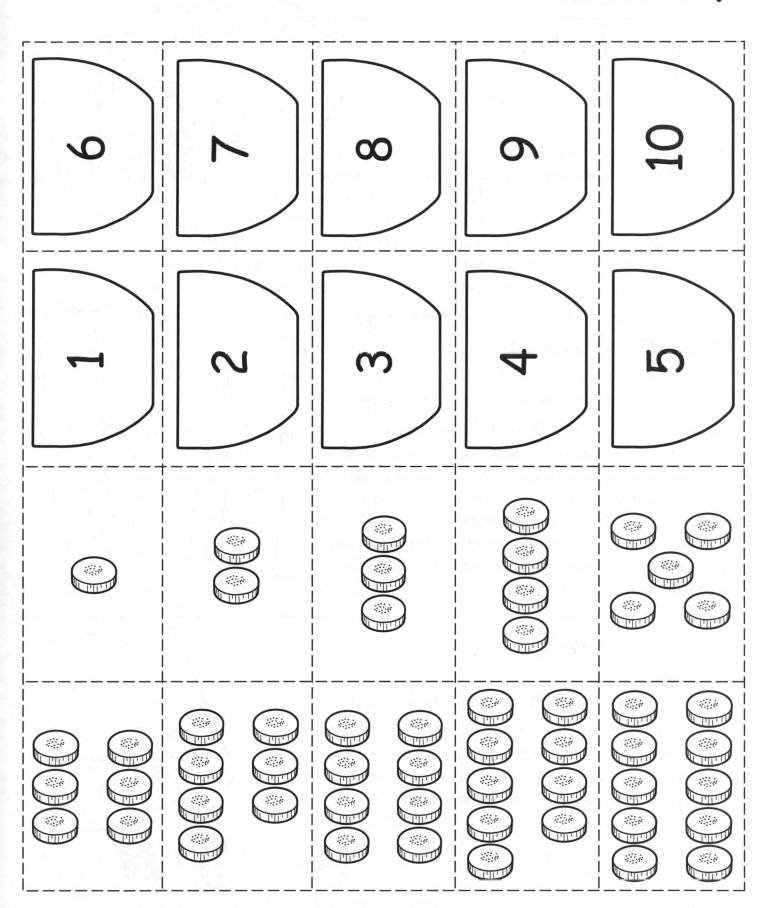

Popsicle Days

Popsicle Match

Materials:

folder, construction paper, scissors, glue, envelope, crayons or makers

Reproduce two sets of Popsicle cards (page 57). Program one set of cards with a color word (red, blue, yellow, green, orange, purple, pink, gray, white, black) and glue onto the inside of a folder. Use a matching color crayon to color each of the remaining cards. Decorate, then write Popsicle Match on the front of the folder. Glue an envelope to the back of the folder for card storage. To practice matching, children remove all cards from the envelope to sort and place a matching color Popsicle on each color word Popsicle.

Popsicle Puzzles

Materials:

folder, oak tag, crayons or markers, scissors, glue, envelope

Decorate the front of a file folder with shapes cut from construction paper. Write Popsicle Puzzles on the folder. Reproduce, program, color, and cut apart Popsicle puzzles (page 58) with shapes as shown. Glue one half of each Popsicle puzzle on the inside of the folder. Glue an envelope to the back of the folder to store puzzle halves. To practice matching shapes, children remove all puzzle halves from the envelope to sort and place each Popsicle half beside its match.

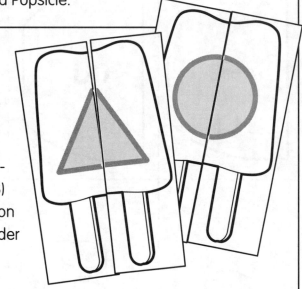

Paint a Popsicle

Materials:

oak tag, scissors, glue, paint, brushes, construction paper

Reproduce a large oak tag Popsicle (page 58) for each child to cut out. Prepare a work station with brushes, and paint for children to paint their Popsicles. When the paint has dried, mount each child's Popsicle on a sheet of colored construction paper. Write each child's name on the back of his or her Popsicle.

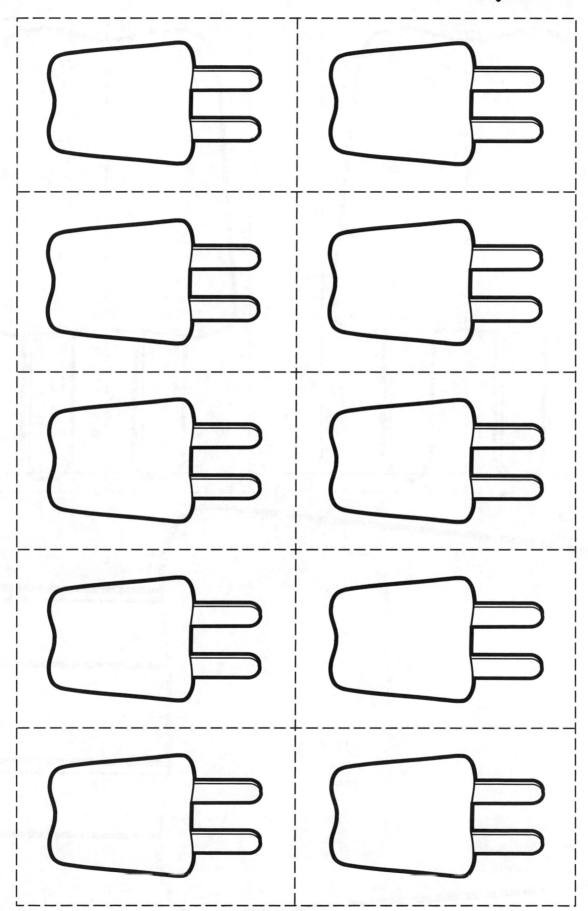

Popsicle Days

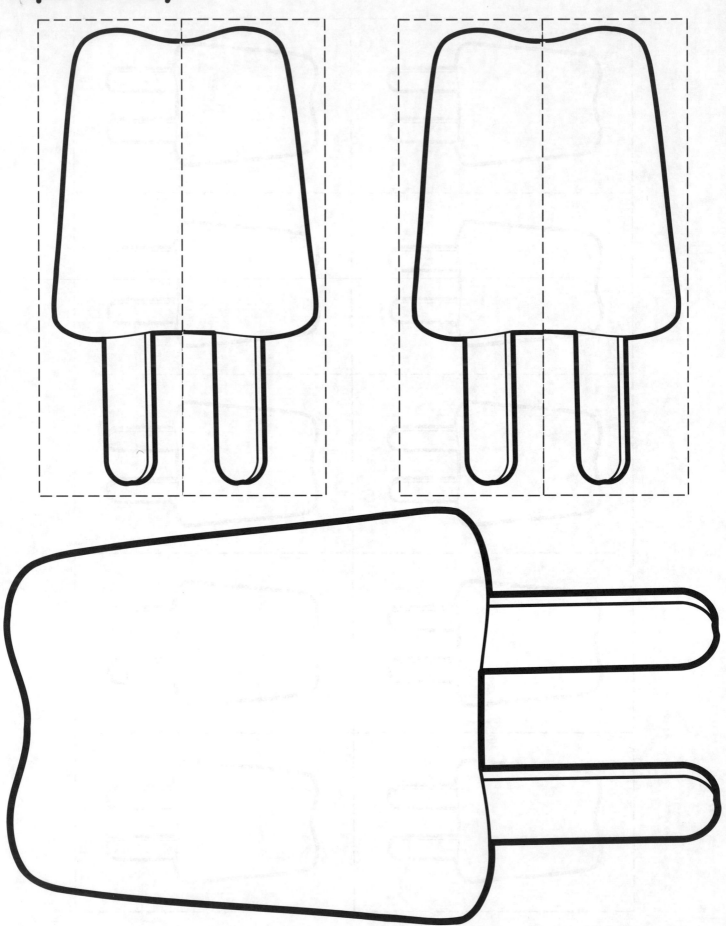

Horseshoe Concentration

Materials:

construction paper, crayons or markers, scissors, plastic bag

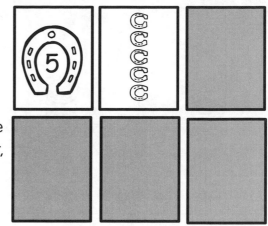

Reproduce, color, laminate, and cut apart a set of construction paper horseshoe cards (page 60). Show how to shuffle and place all the cards, face down, on a flat surface. Then have each player, in turn, turn over two cards to find a match. If there is a match, the player keeps the cards. If there is no match, the cards are turned back over, and the next player takes his or her turn. Play continues until all cards are matched. Store cards in a resealable plastic bag when not in use. Reproduce a set of cards for each child for a take-home matching activity.

Horseshoe Mobile

Materials:

crayons or markers, scissors, glue, construction paper, stapler, yarn

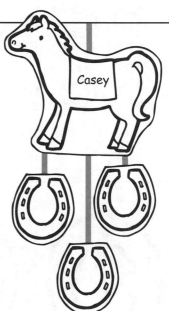

Reproduce horse and horseshoe patterns (page 61) for children to make mobiles. Have children color and cut out a horse and horseshoes. Help each child arrange the horse and horseshoes into a mobile design of his or her choice. Staple a length of yarn to the back of each horseshoe, then to the horse. Write each child's name on the saddle of his or her horse. Attach a length of yarn to each finished mobile to hang from door and window casings or from the ceiling.

Horses & Shoes Garland

Materials:

oak tag, crayons or markers, scissors, stapler, yarn

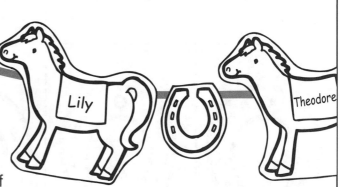

Provide each child with an oak tag horse and horseshoe (page 61) to color and cut out. Help each child write his or her name on the cutouts. Staple each child's horse and horseshoe onto a length of yarn to form a garland. Hang garlands along bulletin board borders or from the bottom of window frames.

Horseshoe Days

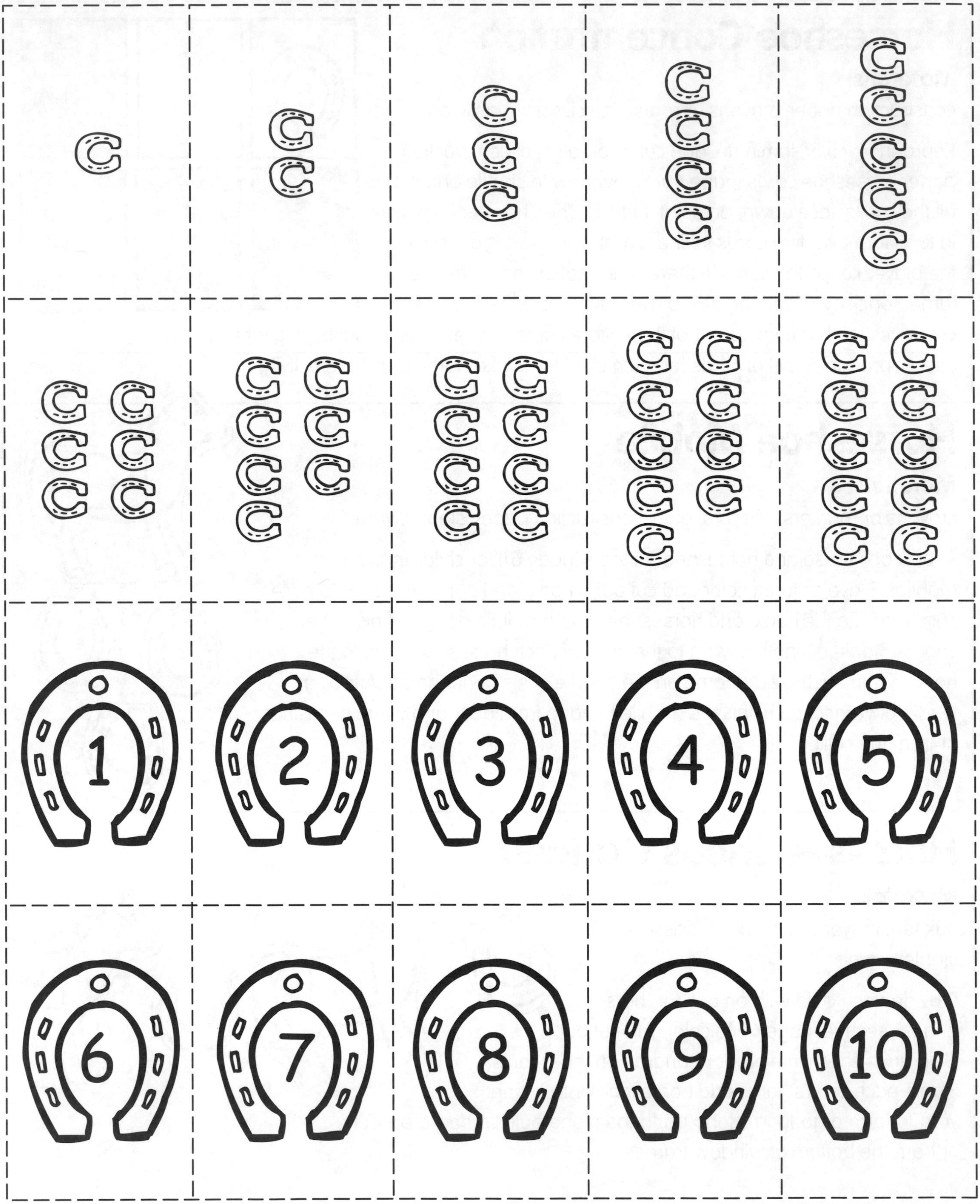

C

C
C

C
C
C

C C
C C
C C

C C
C C
C C
C

C C
C C
C C
C
C

C C
C C
C C
C C

C C
C C
C C
C C

C C
C C
C C
C C
C

C C
C C
C C
C C
C

1 2 3 4 5

6 7 8 9 10

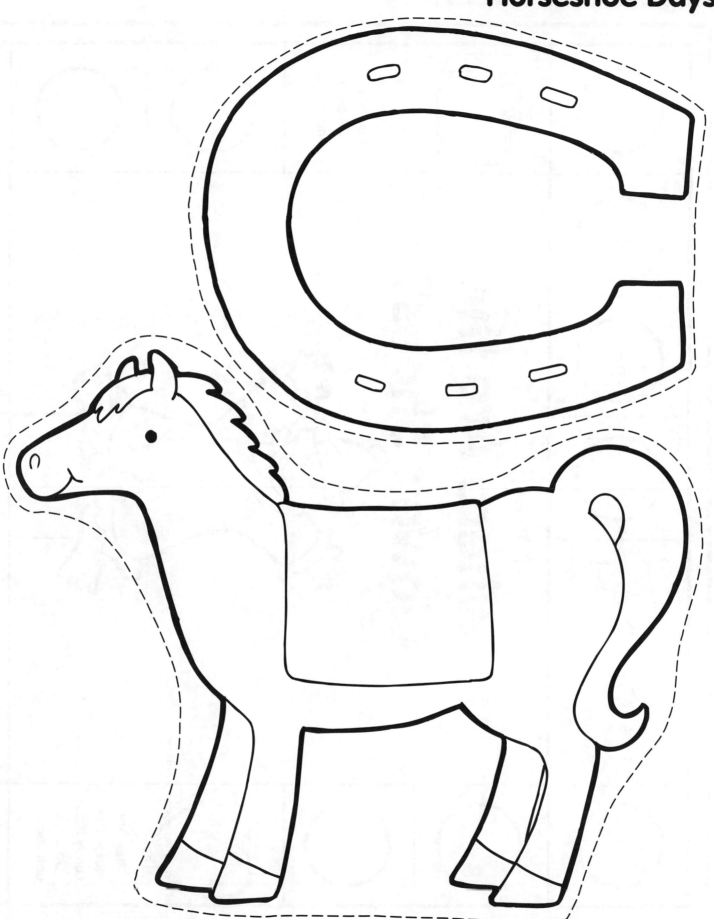

August Game Board

They are not in the lunch box. Go back one space.

They are not in the cardboard box. Go back one space.

Where Are the Clown's Shoes?

They are not in the candy box. Go back one space.

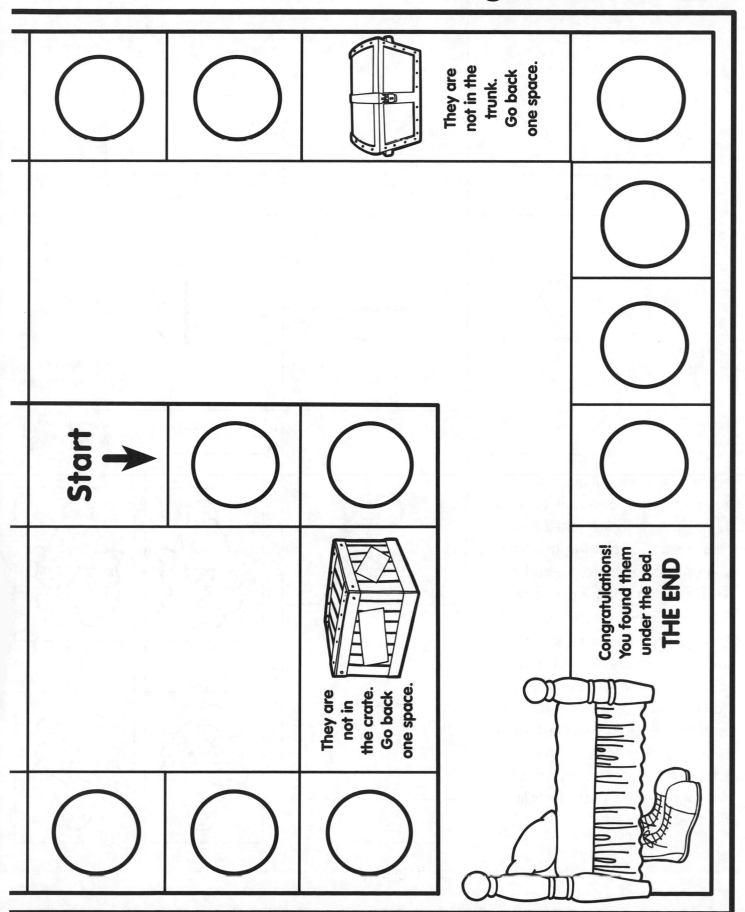

They are not in the trunk. Go back one space.

Start →

They are not in the crate. Go back one space.

Congratulations! You found them under the bed. **THE END**

August Game Pieces

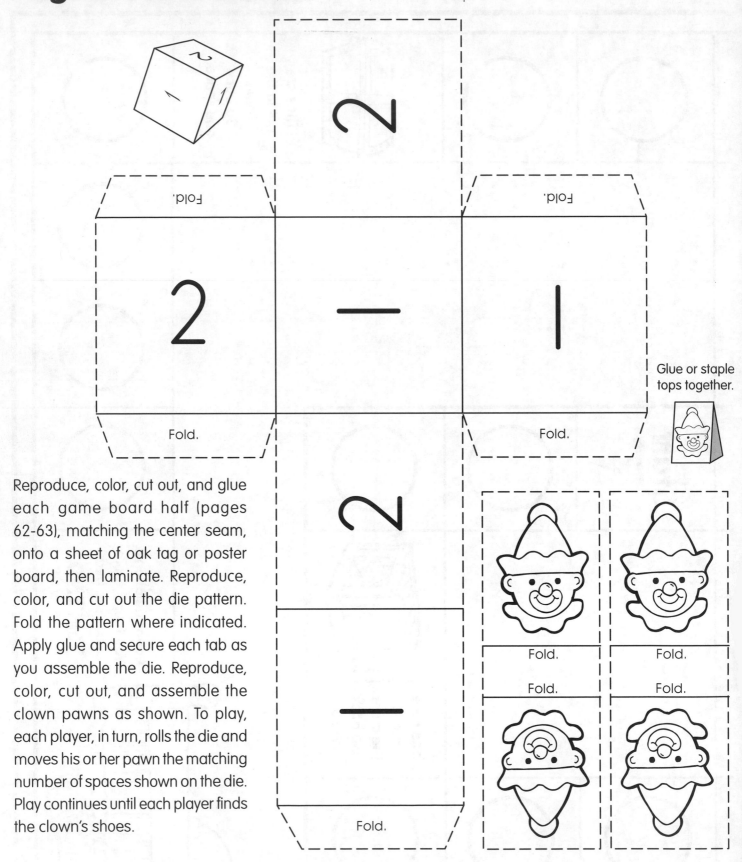

Reproduce, color, cut out, and glue each game board half (pages 62-63), matching the center seam, onto a sheet of oak tag or poster board, then laminate. Reproduce, color, and cut out the die pattern. Fold the pattern where indicated. Apply glue and secure each tab as you assemble the die. Reproduce, color, cut out, and assemble the clown pawns as shown. To play, each player, in turn, rolls the die and moves his or her pawn the matching number of spaces shown on the die. Play continues until each player finds the clown's shoes.